Grannies Homespun Poetry

An amateur poet musing on life

To Pat with best wishes
and hopefully a good read!
love,

Jessie Trudgill   Jess

MARCH 2019.

ISBN:1974603652
ISBN-13:9781974603657

DEDICATION

This book of my writings is dedicated to all my family and friends who have encouraged me to have the confidence to share them with a wider audience.

.

CONTENTS

ACKNOWLEDGMENTS

I would like to acknowledge the help of my Grand-daughter Emily who has painstakingly typed up the contents of this book from handwritten notes on scraps of paper and together with her father has managed to put them in some kind of order.
I would like to thank Ralph for his tireless help and support of my efforts and for putting my writings onto the Audlem Village website. Also everyone in the village who welcomed me upon my arrival after I moved here some years ago. I have had the good fortune to make some great friends.
Thanks also to all the people I have met over the years who have given me inspiration and in many cases have been the seeds from which this book has grown.

1 PEOPLE

I Read This Saying Somewhere

"People walk through our lives.
But only friends leave their
footprints on our hearts."

A Friend

I have a friend. She's very special
I only met her a few months ago
She has made me realise how much I needed
A friend when I was feeling low.

She's fun to be with, she makes me laugh
Because that is what we do
We laugh, we chat and we walk –
Not just a stroll, we go a mile or two.

Whenever the weather is kind
We go along beside the canal
We never know who and what we'll find
But there's always someone to smile at -
And mostly they smile back.

After parting with my friends so far away
My days would drag
But now I'm glad
And look forward to another day

There's no one quite like a good pal
And she's that -
There to help and there to care
With any luck our future days
Will be - set fair

Amy Johnson

She stood on the headland, this slip of a girl
Her head in the clouds, her mind in a whirl
The wind it was blowing, both this way and that
It seemed to desire her little red hat.

She didn't notice, she seemed not to care
She was watching the birds flying high in the air
How was it she wondered, what was the thrill?
Soaring high in the sky – it fair made her ill!

The waves were so angry, they crashed and they roared
Noisily determined not to be ignored
They made no impact on this chip of a girl
With her head in the clouds and her mind in a whirl.

She knew what she wanted, her future looked bright
She had studied for years both day and by night
She would succeed, she was sure of that
As she held on tight to her little red hat.

All she needed right now was the right kind of luck
All her family and friends said she had what it took,
To fulfill all her dreams, her desires and her needs
But it was all up to her if was to succeed.

This was the year she was sure of that
As she tightened hold of her little red hat
It was 1930, not the twenties anymore
It was the year, she was sure, for her to open the door.

For the future, for females, for history to be made!
To give herself, this slip of a girl, a bright accolade.
There would be troubles ahead, she was sure of that
As the wind whisked away her little red hat

Now it's 2016 and we are rather blasé –
We've had men on the moon and it's easy to say
In those years we've come a long way.
Yes, we must be sure of that –

But we mustn't forget that slip of a girl in the little red hat
She rates among the famous, the daring and the brave
And she did make history and she got her accolade.
She's up there somewhere, where the wild winds whirl
This wizard woman, this slip of a girl.

Dame Vera Lynn O.B.E

She was only 7years old
When she made her debut,
Singing, even then,
With her heart as well as her voice
What a talent!

We all know her.
She was the forces sweetheart
And what a sweetheart she became
What a girl!

She helped win the war
It has often been said
For, wherever our forces went
She was with them – in song
Bringing tender thoughts of home
Giving them a will to carry on
What a women!

When she became a member of E.N.S.A
She left our shores
To entertain our lassies and our lads.
Going to Egypt, India and Burma –
Receiving the Burma Star
For her bravery when things looked bad
And for her contribution to morale
What a gal!

To the folks back at home
She brought hope.
Showed us how to smile through our tears
She gave us a reason to carry on too,
Lifting our hearts with her songs
What a darling!

To those who suffered bombing and deprivation
And for those who suffered loss
She gave a belief in a future.
What a sweetheart!

What a lady, what a woman.
A songbird, - a wife, - a mother –
A treasure.
Never to be forgotten.

A Name

Many, many moons ago
In days long gone,
When I was only a bairn
I had a "bestest" friend
Who lived at the end of our road.

She came from a far off land
Way, way across the sea
But we became the best of friends,
She and me

But the war came and cut asunder
Our young friendship
So where is she now, I wonder?
Is she back, back in that land across the sea?

I remember her
As if it were yesterday
Will she ever think of me?
I will never find out – never know,
Just let it be – let it be –
Just another memory

I recall, quite clearly, her name
No nickname, no shortened names for her
She was – Kathleen Mary Teresa Donlevy McDonald

She was very proud
She liked her name
And I liked her.

Stapleton Cotton – The Lord Combermere
1st Viscount Combermere

This man was colourful, gallant and brave
He lived his life to the full
Fearless under fire
No matter how dire

He was a gentleman
Born the 2nd son of a Baronet
1773 was the year of his birth
A very special year
Educated at Westminster School
Always fearless, flamboyant but fair

He married three times
Each lady an aristocrat
In her own right
6 children blessed his life
2 were lost in infancy
Lost without a fight

He was wounded, bloodied
But disheartened never
He was fearless in danger
To him, danger was his life
Always fearless, flamboyant but fair

His life it seems
Was a life worth living
91 years he lived his dreams
Maybe his phantoms, we just don't know

A gentleman to revere
A man for all seasons in every way
A man to admire
Always fearless, flamboyant but fair

Ode To Susan Sellers,
The High Sheriff Of Cheshire

We had a lady visit us a week or two ago
A very special lady, we were told
When we heard this news we were excited
But apprehensive to say the least

When our 'Special Lady' arrived
She looked very striking in her regalia
We didn't expect someone quite as important
As the High Sheriff of Cheshire

She delighted us with her charm and dignity
Shaking hands with everyone in turn
Speaking to us all
She was welcomed very warmly
By Ronni and Roger
When she had settled down
Ronni handed her a cuppa -
Very welcome I expect

She told us all about her attire
Telling first, why her lovely hat
Was adorned with ostrich feathers -
Quite large feathers, as you can imagine

Well, it seems long long ago when battles raged
Ostrich's were let loose onto the battle fields
After furious fighting
They would tidy up the area
By eating everything in sight
Seems Ostrich's never suffer from indigestion

Her smart navy suit was handmade for her
She borrowed her hat
The bright buttons on sleeves and jacket
Were from her R.A.F uniform – just the thing
Ruffles at her throat and cuffs
The final touch
She also had a velvet cape
I must not forget that

This was her first visit to Audlem
And she seemed to like it very much
We agree, it's the place to be

She was a very good storyteller
Enabling us to imagine
Life in the 'days of old'
1000 years to be exact
When Sheriffs were first appointed by royalty
The oldest continuous secular office under the crown

She has had a busy year in office
Visiting towns and villages
Supporting charities, going to community centres
Police stations, Schools and Prisons
Also assuring the good welfare of visiting court judges
Offering them hospitality
All part of her role as High Sheriff

We really did enjoy her visit
It gave us food for thought
And much to talk about

Cheerio Ronni

I have been asked to write you this little something
Because we need you to know our sad feelings
We will so miss you Ronni, you with your happy smile
Your helping hands, your listening ear
And of course your ability to cope with us all!

You have been a close friend, week after week
A friend to everyone in the ADCA Tuesday gathering
And the Friday morning coffee club

All of us agree, we cannot fault you in any way
You cook like an artist, you watch over us always
Noticing if there is anything wrong, and,
You deal with such an occurrence
With tenderness and understanding

We hope to see you, now and then
Even if you are not at our beck and call
Please do not forget our little band of 'oldies'
Pop in, smile, have a chat – and make our day.
Though these lines seem a bit cheesy
We mean every word

Have a happy retirement
Enjoy every moment with your family
They will have you to themselves
Lovely jubbly!

2 MY SELF

Home and Glory

I'm watching television on a very special day
But I've tears in my eyes
Tears of emotion, not sadness
I'm watching the Diamond Jubilee water pageant
For the Queen, our Queen.

Just sitting in my little room
All by myself
But I've been everywhere today
And lived every moment, seen sights
Heard wonderful interview stories.

Children in the high street, waving their flags
Lots of red, white and blue
Everyone beaming with pride and joy
Families bound together like glue
Mums and Dads, Girls and Boys.

I've seen many uniforms
And outfits to fit the occasion
Raincoats too, but no one seems to care
Plenty of noise, cheers and excitement
All from my little room, all by myself.

I'm just a mother and a gran
Proud to be British, the best way I can
Glad to be here on this special day
With tears in my eyes,
I was watching too, when it all began
60 years ago
But in someone else's little room.

Words

Glishy is a lovely word
And so is lollipop
I have so many words I like
I don't know when to stop

There's lickety-split and lemonade
Lemons, loopy and woggles
Toggles too, and lucozade
Sometimes my mind just boggles

Lost and lonely, I don't like
But there's always bright and breezy
Sneezy and wheezy come to mind
It sounds so very easy

This and that and click and clack
Lavender water and Calvin Klein
Bric-a-brac and jumble
But the best word for me
Must be – love.
For all time

Perhaps

I like to write poems
I don't quite know why –
I was never good at English
And poetry passed me by.

I show them to my husband
Friends and family too
They nod and smile, as if to say
"They're very good, now go away"

I'm just a jotting poet
No Keats or Shelly – me
I while away some happy hours
In my land of fantasy

I have no dreams of fortune
No hopes of lifelong fame
Perhaps a mention in a book -
And beneath it find my name.

Becoming Old – The Ladies Way

Why can't our skin stay smooth and bright?
Why do we have to get wrinkly when we get old?
Why do some ladies get whiskers?
With the beginnings of a beard appearing overnight.
It seems a bit unfair.

When I was young and flighty
I never thought about getting old –
Never put cream on nightly
Never thought I would get old –
Another Peter Pan

I remember looking at ladies with whiskers
When I was young
And thought it was fun
Now it's me being scrutinized
And I don't like it!

Take it from me
I enjoy being old
And because I'm still quite vain
I keep my tweezers handy
And my pot of cream.

But how I wish I could be young again.

On These We Stand

My feet are a disaster zone!
I have more corns than I have toes
And my nails have a mind of their own.
Shall I be thick? Or shall I be thin? –
Depends, I think, on what mood they're in.

There once was a time when my feet were sublime,
But to add to my woe I've a sore
Hammer toe!

My feet are not pretty –
They have altered in shape and in size.
Each one, sad to say,
Is a sight for sore eyes!

They have stood the test of time,
Ha Ha!
But now, with cracks on my heels,
I'd be much better off with a pair of wheels!

Tents and Wigwams

My oh my. Me and my winceyette nighties
A sight to behold
What it is to be old!

Once upon a time I wore
Short, pretty, girly nighties
But now, I admit
It's warmth I desire
Not to be the object of desire!

I don't hang them on the line
Outside to dry –
The sight of them
Only makes me want to cry!

I hang them indoor
In a warm corner somewhere
And I try my best
To forget they are there.

These bloody shapeless things
I pretend they're not mine!

But of course they are mine,
And I'm truly thankful they are –
I don't need charm to keep me warm!

I have a duvet-
My blanket is switched on. So –
Snuggled up tight and wearing my nightie
I'm soon in the lad of nod!

A Waste Of Time

He stood in the spotlight
This gorgeous young man
With green eyes and black hair
My kind of man
But he never saw me – never knew I was there.

I sat and waited
For him to finish his song.
I knew from the past
It wouldn't take long.

For I've been a fan
Of this gorgeous young man
For many a month
Perhaps even years.
Pulling my heart strings
And bringing on tears

Why doesn't he see me
Why doesn't he know –

That I love him.

What Will Be-Will Be

Was it only yesterday?
When I was young and fancy free? –
It seems so very long ago – to me!

There was a time,
A time sublime
When all I wanted and needed
Was then and there
I had no worries – not even a care!

Now, all I have to think about is –
How long will my future be?
I tell myself "you silly old moo,
It will last as long as you do, -
So, make the most of the time you have."
And that is what I aim to do.

Who can tell, so I don't dwell
I've had a good life –
Certainly lived it!
As all who know me
And love me – will agree!

There have been regrets,
Some I'd rather forget –
Life goes on – I hope –
For a good while yet.

So with this thought in mind
I'll live it with style, my style
However long it lasts.

The Last Straw

I woke up this morning –
Not my usual self,
I must have been dreaming I think
I just didn't feel quite "in the pink"

The washing machine was spinning the very last spin
So that helped, a little, the mood I was in.
I said to myself, as I looked at the sky
My washing this morning, is bound to get dry

So I put most of it out on the washing line

The towels, they were blowing in the breeze
So I decided to hang out the rest.
Then – disaster struck – the line – it broke!
Leaving my clean washing around my knees

Later I had my lunch, still feeling low,
Then I thought – I know-
I'll have a glass of sherry!
That's sure to make me merry.
No luck, no avail
I still feel like having a good old wail

I need a tonic, yes, I'm sure I do
With some gin, -
Just to improve the mood I'm in!
I know I have a bottle, hidden away.
Then I'll leave buying a new line
For another day.

Memories

I'm on my own today
So I have the tele on
To keep myself company.
I'm not really watching
I'm daydreaming of days long gone.

Memories come flooding back
Some make me smile to myself
But, now and then,
I smile where a smile should be!

Some make me sad
And I'm wondering why
I keep them through the years –
But they are mine
And well worth keeping.

Each of us reminisce
Remembering, perhaps, our first kiss?
Our very first love?
How many moons have waxed and waned since.

Those long gone
We remember –
We see them
So clear, so new –
Tucked away. Forgotten – never!

We can "play" our memories
Over and over –
Memories, memories, memories.

Germ Attack

I've got a cold
My bones, they ache
My eyes are sore
And so is my throat!
I don't think there's much hope for me –
I'm just a moaning misery

My friends are keeping well away
I feel like I've been abandoned!

The tele is on to cheer me
But I'm not in the mood
For soaps and such
Apart from them, there's nothing much
So I'm off to bed –

I know, I'll have a hot toddy!
Take it up to my room, to enjoy –
That thought has cheered me up!
Will make me sleep as well, you know
Even if I ache from head to toe!

Tomorrow is another day.

Sometimes

I'm sometimes tired of just being me
But who do I really want to be?
No one special comes to mind
Cos really I'm just the simple kind.

Each morning, when I open my eyes
I try at once to visualize,
Could I have been a femme – fatale?
Surely not for this old gal.

Maybe I'd like to air my views
On income tax and revenues.
Go to meetings and strut and shout
And hope I know what I'm talking about!

I take a look at my life again
And liken it to a picture frame.
It holds within a moment past –
Gone forever, but there to last.

A life of Riley is everyone's dream
But sometimes that's not all it seems.
I think I'll stay just as I am
And get on with making that strawberry jam!

An Occasion

I'm going out
For afternoon tea today
I've not had an invitation –
But I'm going anyway!

It will be quite an occasion
I'm sure of that!
I'll wear my best bib and tucker
But I'll not be wearing a hat!

There's sure to be a sarnie selection
"Dainty like" – with no crusts!
Set out with perfection
On willow patterned plates.

I won't be late
It's not far away
It will only take me a jiffy
To be on my way.

I'm getting closer now –
Ah! I've arrived!

Better take off my pinny
And use a serviette!
Cos there's only me at this party
Me and the birds and the bees

It's good, now and then
To do things "Properlike"
And not with a tray on my knees –
"lazylike"

3. THE MONTHS OF THE YEAR

January

A happy new year to one and all,
Old or new, short or tall
This is my new wish to you.
It's January – A new month
A new year.

We all know January
Is a very cold month.
So why not snuggle up close
To those we love –
Be bold – Not cold!

These chilly nights
And bitter cold days
With snow, frost and icy blasts
Are bound to last –
For quite a while,
We know this to our cost.

So, with our scarves, hats and woolly gloves
To keep us warm
And keep out the cold
We'll set about our business
And come to no harm.

Just put our best foot forward, smile,
And carry on – as usual.

February

Here we are, here we are,
Here we are again.
Happy as can be,
All good friends
And jolly good company.

Never mind the weather,
Never mind the rain,
The gales, the frost or the snow –
Because we have a special day this month
And that should ease the pain.

We have Valentines Day!
A romantic day with a capital "R".
Romance is in the air.
Valentine cards everywhere –
To send to our loved ones –
Secretly of course!

There are red roses to buy,
Boxes and boxes of chocolates
Tied up with big red bows.
Notes with loving wishes,
Poems too – but only to be signed
"From me to you"

Don't let the weather get you down
Don't wear a frown
Look to march – wearing it's mantle of Spring.

(With apologies to the writers and composers of the original song 'here
we are again' Charles Knight & Kenneth Lyle)

Magical March

March is a special month for me
It is when we begin to smile
Put away that gloom and doom
Begin to walk that extra mile through life

March holds the key which unlocks the door
To warm sunshine and soft Spring breezes.
Perhaps the end to coughs and sneezes!

God's young creatures gambol and leap
With sheer delight,
And the whole world takes on
A brighter light.

This month of magic and of mystery
Is full of expectation,
High hopes and future plans –
For thee and for me.

It's a month when –
Mother Nature pulls out all the stops,
Puts on her clogs
And brings forth new life.

March may come in like a lion
And go out like a lamb (or vice versa)
But I like March –
I am who I am – a mad March Hare!

By the way – don't forget to say
"White Rabbits"

April

What a lovely month April can be
Now that March has left us well into spring
When love is in the air
Hopefully not just for the birds and bees!

Flowers bloom
Trees are no longer bare
Clothed now, with opening buds
And blossom
If only we could find the time
To stand and stare –
Mother Nature at her best.

The sun is beginning to gleam
And there's warmth in "them thar" beams
So all we need to do now – is –
Spring clean!

Do the garden –
Get rid of the weeds –
Plant the veg
Paint the fence, mend the shed
But best of all, it has to be said,
Book a holiday!

Don't worry if you get caught out
And become an April Fool –
It's just a game we played at school – Remember
Those happy days, carefree days,
Silly days, but not to be forgotten days.
Oh, to be young again –
Young at heart.

May

It's May time, its May time
When birds do sing
A ring ding ding
Sweet lovers love the spring

Yes the month of May is here
And so is the May blossom!
So the question is: -
Do we cast a clout at the end of the month?
Or when the May blossom chooses to appear.
I wonder? – Never Mind
We have a very exciting
Month ahead of us
In Audlem
We have our arts and music festival
So this means a busy month
For all of us.

It's when the whole village
Comes alive
With visitors – music and singing
And art of every genre.

Then, when the festival comes to an end
We have our Carnival Day!

Audlem is certainly
The place to be – especially
In the marvelous
Month of May.

June

I'm late, I'm late
For a very important date
No time to waste
Hello – Goodbye
It's June, It's June, It's June
So, enjoy, enjoy, enjoy

Yes it is June,
"Flaming June"
The month we can expect
Some sunny days at last!

Let's hope for better climes
Perhaps not wall to wall sun,
But clear blue skies,
Warm breezes
But perhaps just a few drops of rain.

This is the month for weddings,
As the saying goes –
"Happy is the Bride.
The sun shines on today"
So we need plenty of sunshine
And a lot of happy brides.

This may not be a poem
-As such
But I haven't had the time
To make it all Rhyme

Sorry!

July

Here comes summer! Hurray –
Six months of the year
Have just flown by
And now we have July –
A month of blue skies
And balmy days.

In the cool of the evening air
We can sit outside, have a BBQ
Chat, read have a tipple or two –
Naughty but nice.
Remember a little of what you fancy
Does you good – and that's a fact!

The gardens are at their best
Fruit trees bursting with newly born fruit
And there's an abundance of soft fruit to be had
So really, July can't be bad!

We know it's not a good time for all
Hay fever is a pest!
But it will pass,
Just keep the hankies at the ready –
I do!

This month, we have, here in Audlem,
Our picnic in the park to enjoy
And the great Festival of Transport
Exciting times!

August

A month just waiting to surprise us
In many many ways.
A promise of more sunshine perhaps
Just to enjoy
While we still have long days.

And August is a bountiful month
Plenty of fruit and veg.
In gardens, on trees and in the hedgerows.
They supply us with the best!

So pick what you can,
Eat what you can,
Then freeze, bottle or preserve the rest
If there's anything left behind –
That is!
And, if you have the mind!

Because: -
In the midst of winter
What do you crave –?
Besides the warmth of the sun
A taste of summer – a morsel
Hand-picked or grown.

Back to the month of August –
This is the time to take care,
When those boozy, woozy wasps,
Drunk with the juice of the fruit,
Are on the wing,
Declaring war!
And they 'don't Arf' give a nasty sting!

September

When will apples be ready to eat
And the plums be ripe?
September

When are the pears at their best
And the brambles dripping with juice?
September

When do the swallows leave home
For distant climes?
September

When does the sun lose its warmth?
And the breezes cool?
September

Bountiful September

October (1)

Chimneys smoke and there's
Frost in the air
And leaves fall from the trees
Without so much as a care

Gloves, scarves and woolly hats are
The order of the day
To keep us warm, as we go on our way.

October (2)

October is full of mystery and magic
There's a weird and wonderful night to be had

When witches, hobgoblins, ghosts and ghouls
Come out to play – but they're really not bad

They want goodies and pennies and maybe a sweet
It's good to be young and play trick or treat.

November – A Month to Remember

Yes, there are many dates
To remember this month
One, in particular
Must not be forgot!
November the 5th of course
Gunpowder, treason and plot.

Displays are planned
Throughout the land
By villages and towns
Bonfires are built –
But not lit-just waiting.

Fireworks are bought
And put away
For safety
Until that very special day.

Through windows clear
Eager young families watch
While Dad lights up the sparklers
Such excitement! Without a tear!

Remember too –
November will be cold and wet
But if we wrap up warm
And take a brolly,
We should be here
To greet December,
With its Mistletoe and Holly!

December

Without love in our lives
Life just isn't worth a jot
Just sit a while and wonder why

We can't be happy with our lot
Remember, the best things in life are free
For friends and neighbours, you and me
For others too, both near and far
We need to try and follow that star

Life is what we make it

Anthology for December

-December, Advent and Christmas
There's much going on this time of the year
Because December is the month of Christmas
The birthday of our Lord. A celebration.
A time to reflect,
Count our blessings and give thanks.

-But
It's also a special time of the year
For the young, and the young at heart!
A delightful month, exciting, joyful,
Full of wishes, hope and dreams
For all.

-And
For those who have seen many Decembers,
Just sit a while
And remember those Christmases,
And the years in between.
Be thankful, be glad
Smile, be happy, not sad.

-December
A busy month, an expensive month,
Nevertheless, a special month.
Shops are bright with fairy lights
To cheer us through the long dark nights.

-Then
When all is 'done and dusted'
Planned, bought and paid for
Sit back relax, blow the expense!
We're still here so –
Lap it up, the whole darned lot
Don't be the one Santa forgot.

LIVE, LOVE AND ENJOY
HAPPY CHRISTMAS!

End of Year Thoughts

It's raining again
Raindrops are hitting the windows
Not falling on my head!
I'm glad to be indoors.

It's nearing the end of the year
Another year has almost
'Bitten the dust' —
As the saying goes.

What will January Bring?
And the following 11 months
Who knows?
We'll find out eventually.

We will just live, love and be happy,
Healthy, we hope and possibly wealthy.

We have our memories,
Our dreams and our faith.
We are who we are
And always will be!
Glad to be alive.

These are just some thoughts
I have on a cold December 'noon.

4 THE SEASONS OF THE YEAR

Trumpeting The Spring

I saw them standing upon the grass
As I walked towards the church
They were standing proud like soldiers, soldiers of the earth-
Daffodils

I was dressed for the winter
And shivering in the wind
They were clothed in green,
And not long born
But dancing in the breeze –
Daffodils

Among them, peeping –
Standing – bright as buttons –
Cheeky little faces
Looking up at me –
Daisies

Nature at her very best
Unveiling her spring collection

Jessie Trudgill

Spring

Green shoots adorn the hedgerows
And there's blossom on the trees
Cotton wool clouds float in a sky of blue
Blown there by a gentle breeze
The days grow longer and warmer too
So there's plenty to plan in the garden
And certainly plenty to do!

Summer Thoughts

"Summer" is a dreamy word
A happy word. A warm word,
An exciting word.
A word which conjures up delight.

Delight at the thought of a holiday –
The thought of 'no school' for a few weeks.
A thought of long rides into the country.
A walk, early morning,
With only bird song for company!

A summer 'get together' with friends and neighbors.
Perhaps a family BBQ.
Romantic walks in the cool evening air,
With a loved one, hand in hand

Summer is when winter attire is stowed away,
And light, airy clothes, donned.
Sandals and bare feet – what a treat!

Whatever summer has in store
And whatever it holds for us,
We will enjoy ourselves, -
Relax on our hols or at home,
In the garden – happy long days.

Summer beckons a happy time for all –
Hopefully

Autumn

Autumn, to me, is a closing down time…
Rather like a shop – but without a written sign!
If it were to have a sign, I'm sure it would read –
'Closing Down – due to the season –
Opening again in the spring'

It is a time when the trees
Begin to lose their summer glory
Greens, turning into hues of yellow, brown and gold
Leaves fall – the trees become skeletal –
With a beauty of their own,
Outlined against the skyline –
An artist's delight.

Flowers wilt, their days numbered
And all animals don their winter coasts –
Mother Nature playing her part.

We ourselves begin to feel the chill
The wind, no longer a breeze
Whistles down the dale and hill
As if to say "we're here,
And we're here to stay"

The nights are drawing in, fast now.
The house seems cold! "Put on a duvet, and
Shut that door", we begin to say!

We know there is reason for this season
We just wait for Mother Nature
To deliver winter –
And our future.

Dancing Leaves

Glancing through my window
It looked a dreary day.
Lots of heavy, low clouds – brooding.
Not the best of views.

I turned away for a while
Only to return, later –
To see, almost, the same gloom
I watched for a moment or two –

Then, what caught my eye
Just made me smile
Cheered me up, somehow.

There, coming along the road
Towards the house
Were dozens and dozens
Of nut brown leaves!

Waltzing along in the brisk breeze
Not in any particular style,
Just twisting and turning, at will.

Not just waltzing, - leaping, jiving
Perhaps quickstep, foxtrotting?
Maybe a Charleston, just for me!
Whatever their music, I didn't care

My imagination gave me free range
A lovely autumn sight – for me.

Winter

White waves and a cold whistling wind
Heavy hovering clouds
Cold sleeting rain
This means winter

Early dark nights call for early to bed
Dark morning, wishes for a long lie in
Thick duvets and bed socks
This means winter

Cold feet or cosy slippers
An easy choice to make
Hats, scarves and woolly gloves
This means winter

Winter comes with all its glory
Bringing with it a fresh promise of snow
There's a nip in the air and frost on the ground
But we can cope – we usually do,
Because spring is just around the corner!

Jessie's Winter Poem.

Another season ahead of us
Another season fades
We all know cold weather approaches
This is the season we call winter!

It advances with a chill
A chill almost beyond compare
With its bleak, cold, frigid
Scant, freezing and gelid air

It comes with a beauty
If we can look further –
The hoar frosts appear.
Laying, clinging, upon the countryside.
Hedges, walls, trees, a true wonder,
Beauty, once more at its best –
Thanks to Mother Nature.

As the age old annals tell us –
"After a hoar frost expect rain"
Some truth in this!
But we will wait and see
If this one is true –
"A ring around the moon
On a clear, bright night
Means snow"

The air before the snow,
Becomes still, quiet,
Then soft feathery flakes began to fall,
Floating slowly at first, settling, everywhere in sight,
Turning the land into a carpet of white.
Winter is coming –
Let us all enjoy!

Christmas Greetings

Wherever did I put my Christmas card book?
Friends and family are all in there
I've tried the cupboards – everywhere –
There's nowhere else to look!
It seems no time since I put it away
In readiness for another day
Ah, yes. It's found, so I'll proceed
I write the names on this year's list
I'm truly thankful there's none to be missed
Some to be added as families grow
And new friends I've had the pleasure to know
When all is 'Done and dusted' as they say
I write my cards, wish them god speed and send them on their way
Hoping they bring health and happiness to one and all
So it's happy Christmas and God bless from Jess

My Christmas Visitor

I had a little friend visit me this Christmas
It never speaks. And it moves from place to place.
It came from nowhere- just seemed to appear
I speak to it often – even wished it a Happy New Year!

(I must try to get out more!)

I can't feed it. It doesn't seem to eat
It has feelers, wings and little sticky feet
It uses its feet to cling to the wall
And is dark brown in colour and about 1 inch tall.

Its wings, when opened are a beautiful sight
All the colours of the rainbow, bright, bright, bright
A lovely wonder to behold –
One I'll remember as I grow old.

All God's creatures have a life span
And I know it can't last forever
But I'll enjoy my little visitor
While I can

My Beautiful Christmas Butterfly.

My Beautiful Christmas Butterfly
My little Christmas visitor is no more –
It happened this way

For well over a month
It was my friend
I thought our friendship
Would only end
When it flew away.

With great delight
It supped the honey mix
I left upon a tray
Then vanished – as it were
Into the night
Only to appear
On a bright sunlit day
I was so glad!

But now I'm sad –
For my little friend is dead
I did enjoy my tiny pal
Being here with me
But now it will be –
Flying high
Where the warm breezes blow
In a butterfly sky . . .

Because I know.

After All It Is Christmas

Here we go again
Buying with a frenzy
Spend, spend, spend.

Never mind, what use is money anyway
If it not to be spent!

This is when –
Children of all ages
Are being extra good
Hoping Father Christmas
Will grant their wishes.

But wishes need to be paid for
By those who love them
Family, kith and kin
So we pull out all the stops
Because –
If it were not for us
They would not be here!
Therefore, let us celebrate together and enjoy.
After all, it is Christmas!

This is the time when Jesus was born
A gift from God
Our Saviour, our Lord
Let us not forget –
And give thanks

Jessie Trudgill

5 LIMERICKS

Royal Mail

There was a young postman and sorter,
Who just would not do as he 'aughter'.
He went out in a gale
And lost all of his mail,
And now he's a British rail Porter!

2.5

There once was a lady called Sadie
Who was known to be a bit shady
She would wait for a call
Outside the town hall
And now Sadie's a very rich lady.

A Limerick which just grew and grew.

There was a young Miss from Bordeaux
Who desperately wanted a beau
Tho' she tried and she tried
They all seemed to hide
And she hadn't the chance to say 'NO'.

To the shores of our Fair Isle she came
With intentions of changing her name
A Miss she was now-
'Cos she didn't know how
But a Miss she wouldn't remain.

Tho' the road was a wearisome trail
She decided she MUST find a male,
Not necessarily new –
A second hand one would do
Or perhaps even one in a sale!!

Then one Thursday in March she met Joan
Who said "Cheer up and don't be alone –
Come with me and we'll fly
To the W.I.
And we'll find you a man of your own."

There was Pat in his tatty old hat
And Jack who was short and quite fat
There was Leslie the loser
And Bertie the boozer,
Then along came a milkman named Matt.

I expect you are wondering why
There were men at the W.I.
This fact needs explaining
Or there might be complaining
They were the speakers from March to July!

Now Matt was a very good talker,
Quite handsome, in fact quite a corker,
He could lecture for hours
On tropical flowers
Grown in Mexico, Maine and Minorca.

The end of this tale more or less
Is long overdue, I confess
So it was hard not to shout
When Matt asked her out
And she didn't say 'NO' she said "Yes".!!!
At last ... The End ...

Jessie Trudgill

6 LOVE

Moments

It only takes but a moment
When two in love are there,
It only takes but a moment
A look of love to share

It only takes but a moment
When two in love are apart
It only takes but a moment
To keep your love locked in my heart

It only took but a moment
For me to think up this rhyme
But it will take forever
To love you till the end of time

Togetherness

Holding hands with the one you love
Is like holding on to life
Being with the one you love
Is belonging

Being together
Safe in each other's arms
Is life entwined

A promise made by two
Kept through all the years
Is a challenge

Time is precious
But not everlasting
Love is for life
Let it stand the test of time

My Love

Forever in my mind you'll be
Fast in my memory
Togetherness in the key –
Me for you and you for me

Love?

Love is like an uncut diamond
Plain and uninteresting
Until it meets its beholder
Who sees it in a different light
Then
It glows as if it were facetted,
Cut with many faces.
Warms to the touch, glows with praise.
Precious because it is cosseted,
And becomes a jewel in the crown of life.

Love

Love is unbending
Love has no end
Not to be borrowed
And not to lend

Love can be tarnished
Perhaps even scarred
But love is everlasting
When there's tenderness
And regard

Love has many twists and turns
Along the way
Sometimes it's hard to realise
It's not a game we play

Just look beyond the surface
Of those we love
And accept them as they are
Then love will be everlasting
And it will survive.

A poem to mothers

Remember we all love you
Love you just the way you are.
You may not be perfect –
Perfect is just a whim.
A whim is just thoughts and dreams
Combined with wishes and dreams
Combined with wishes and desires.

So, don't change, don't alter
Don't look for perfection –
Perfection comes from within –
It's you we love and care for.
Remember, to us, you are –
Mother.

7 BITS AND BOBS

A Round To It

'Around to it' – whatever is that?
Is it a jumper or maybe a hat?
Perhaps it's a kettle, all ready for tea
All of us need it, both you and me
There are times in our lives, perhaps now and then
Need to write a letter – but can't find a pen?
Now what an excuse! too lazy it seems
I'll get around to it tomorrow
And get on with my dreams

A Change Of Mind

Coffee is as coffee does
Was what I used to say
Recently I've changed my mind –
Because now I drink Nescafe!

Perfection

If you desire the perfect skin
Be happy with the skin you're in
If you desire the perfect face
Silky smooth, satin and lace
Add rouge and lipstick, red or pink
Whichever colour/shade you think
Be sure your eyes are bright and clear
No mascara smudges anywhere near
Some puffs of powder, here and there
A picture of my lady fair

More Delights And Wishes

A smell of a candle, not long out,
Soup on a cooker and Yorkshire Puds,
Bacon sizzling in a pan and sunny side eggs
Strawberries with cream and apple pies

A starry sky, the man in the moon,
A street light beaming, shadows dancing
Lovers whispering in a shady nook
A comfy cushion, a story book

The sound of a letter as it flops on the mat
A family photo or a tatty old hat
A cuppa with a neighbour and a friendly chat
A wag of a tail, the purr of a cat

A daisy, a buttercup, the buzz of a bee
A chubby baby upon my knee
Teaching a little one, their A.B.C
A bunch of carnations especially for me

What It Means!

Move a lot means getting out of the way.
Moan a lot means never satisfied.
Cry a lot means being miserable.
Sing a lot means happiness.
Read a lot means being a bookworm.
Shout a lot means losing your voice.
Cheat a lot means a bad loser.
Dance a lot means aching feet.
Walk a lot means tired legs.
Write a lot means sore fingers.
Dust a lot means being house-proud.
Wee a lot means wet drawers.
Sleep a lot means happy dreams.
Cook a lot means tasty meals.
Swim a lot means a water baby.
Daydream a lot means happy thoughts.
Smile a lot means others smile with you.
Talk a lot means goodbye to silence.
Worry a lot means more wrinkles.
Eat a lot means gaining weight.
Drink a lot means more trips to the loo.
Smoke a lot means danger.
Kissing a lot means I love you.

Complications

There are things we would like to do
But can't
There are things we don't want to do
But we have them to do
There are dreams to dream
Which never come true
And hopes we hang on to –
Forever

There are plans to be made
Which never see the light of day
So why is life so complicated?
Why can't life just drift along in an easy way
Like the flow of a lazy, a lazy stream?

So much to do – and so little time
But we get there, step by step
Slowly but surely –
Through life.

Questions and Answers

A man said to me
Who won the war?

I said, we did.

How did we manage that?

We had a backbone.

Back bone. What is that?

It's a belief in our country.

Have we still got it?

No.

Why?

Because we're going soft.

What do you mean by that?

We give in to everything
Other countries are ahead of us.

How is that?

Don't ask me - ask the government

They hold the key
For you and me

More Delights

Soapy bubbles, buttons and bows
Fluffy jumpers and comfy shoes
Winding rivers and lapping seas
Flowers waving in a cheeky breeze.

Hot jam tarts and creamy cakes
Silky chocolate, warm marshmallows.
Fizzy pop and frothy coffee
Sticky toffee pudding.
Tinsel on the Christmas tree
Pine needles everywhere
Roast chestnuts and an open fire-
And presents.

Blue skies and sunshine
Stormy clouds, a lightening flash
Moonbeams and butterflies
Snow flakes and rainbows.

Puppy dogs and pussy cats
Creatures great and small
Blue bells and buttercups
Daffodils and daisies.

A well made bed, a warm duvet
A welcome home after a long, long day
A baby's smile, a children's song
A photograph of those long gone.

Dusk in the evening and morning dew
Ribbons and bobbins' of every hue
Good friends, some old, some new.
These are my delights for me and you.

Inspiration

Who needs inspiration? We ladies don't!
We are full of it, need to use it – but when?
Sometimes a 'nudge' in the right direction helps.
There's one way to find that guidance –
That's where the ladies of the W.I. come in!
They will embrace our enthusiasm, kindle our dreams.
Remember, from little ideas – memorable achievements grow!
Helped by the ladies of the W.I. with joint inspiration.
It was these very ladies who gave me belief in myself –
Gave my inspirations 'Free Range.'

8 JUST POEMS

Observations

Where have all the smiles gone
What has happened to conversation
Never get a letter? –
Join the club

No buzz of chatter on a bus
No trivial talk on a train
Just fellow travelers in a trance
As if in another world

Earplugs settled in their place
With trailing wires attached
Mobile phones at the ready
Eyes peering at the screen
Thumbs poised – texting
To whom and to where? –
It makes no odds

We all know the world is changing
And progress is the way
But there was once a day
When passengers looked up –
Smiled, nodded and spoke!

Perhaps I'm old fashioned – thinking this way
But a smile costs nothing and a nod is free
It would make such a difference
To the likes of me

Aftermath

Soldiers marching
Home from war –
Hearts bursting
Hope high, feet sore,
Heads hanging –
Weary all

Thoughts of home –
Rest, warmth.
Family, love.
Smiles, sleep.
Promise, relief.
Waiting, wanting, needing.
Men don't weep

No tears for fallen comrades
Only memories
Forever there –
The futile call of war.

Boots

Yesterday while out for a walk
I saw something
To gladden my heart

First I heard voices
A young voice and a 'grown up' voice
And the clicking of boots
On the pavement –
Coming behind me as I walked

The voices and the clicking boots
Crossed the road
So, I could see them
As well hear them.

There, walking at speed, was a young lad and his dad
The little lad taking the lead

The youngster, wearing with pride
What I imagined to be
A pair of new football boots!
He clutched to his chest – a bottle –
Water, perhaps for half time?

They went towards the playing field
So I lost sight of them both
But I was smiling as I carried on walking,
Thinking of my own lads, when they were young
I even remember the sound of clicking boots!
Where would life be without our memories?

All We Need

Just given time, that's all we need
To put the world to rights.
It's such a shame we can't agree
To put the world to rights

But time runs out, it just won't wait
To put the world to rights.
It's not as if we haven't tried
To put the world to rights,

The times we've tried are etched in blood
To put the world to rights.
With endless talks and endless force
To put the world to rights.

Its heads and hearts and hands we need
To put the world to rights.
Compassion, love and understanding
To put the world to rights.

These combined, mixed well with time
May put the worlds to rights.
Shared out among our fellows man
 Would put the world to rights.

If only this were true.

Women

A glimpse of a woman,
A trace of perfume,
Excites the senses
Of the men in the room.

But women are women
In their own right,
Not just pretty things
To gladden the sight.

Women come in all shapes and sizes
Colour, class and creed
In one way or another
Determined to succeed

There are women who are famous
For the aims they have achieved,
But there are others, who just chug along,
Letting others take the lead.

Women have an intuition
Which makes their world go round,
They're also very clever
Stretching penny into pound,

These many faceted creatures
Aren't merely flesh and bone,
They have a certain mystery –
A mystery all their own.

Women need an understanding
A worthwhile thing to do,
It helps to ease a situation
Should apologies be due!

Women are very special,
Treasures to behold,
Find them and keep them, they're worth their weight in gold!

Bumble Bee Brown Eyes (Song)

Yes, my love he had bumble bee brown eyes,
Eyes that shone with love for me.
I only knew how much I loved him
When he said goodbye to me

I've kept his love locked safely within me,
In my heart he'll always stay.
Beside me near me, always with me
Now, forever and a day.

I've lived my life so far without him
Always hoping one day I'll find
That certain loving, caring someone
To ease my oh so troubled mind!

Yes my love he had bumble bee brown eyes
Eyes that shone with love for me
And if I ever find those brown eyes
I'll keep them shining just for me.

Matilda Jane

There was a girl I knew
She lived not very far from Seaton Carew
Her name, I think was Matilda Jane
All she seemed to want from life
Was to change her name, fortune and fame.

So off to London she went
With only one intent
And that was to find
A rich old gent
Who would love her for her youth alone
And nothing more!

He wouldn't last long; not many years –
Soon to be long gone
Leaving his little wife in tears
That was her plan.

Then, all at once her dream came true
So, of course she knew exactly what to do
When she saw a handsome old git
Which a certain gleam in his eye!

She followed her dream –
Played her game
Became rich, rich, rich.
With plenty of time and money
To wait for fame
When it came along.

Now she's moved to another city
Which to me, is a pity
'Cos she's now in far flung Peru
And that's about all I can tell you
Of Shameless Matilda Jane.

A Secret Place

I have a secret place,
It's hidden inside my head.
This place is mine and mine alone
And no one else must know.

My secret place is where I find
Contentment and peace of mind.
A picture here, a dream or two
Without this place, what would I do?

There's sunshine here and cloudy skies,
Whatever I want I visualize.
Flowers too, and birds and bees
My secret place has all of these.

This place of mine, is mine alone
But all of us can visit
A secret place where no one goes,
Just stop – and think a minute!

Pages

My life has been a magazine,
Rather than a book.
So far so good.
Too late to change it – even if I could.

A book has an ending
I haven't – not yet
I had a beginning
Nobody could forget.

Some smiles, of course along the way
Through many, many years
But since that special day, long gone
I've caused a lot of tears.

I've given love to many
Troubles too and heartbreak,
Like a cake without a candle
There's no icing on *this* cake.

I have some pages yet to turn
I only hope there's many
I have a few more things to do
Costing more than just a penny!

When my magazines is recycled
And I am far away
Please get on with life
And enjoy it, Day by day.

Jessie's Way

My life, so far, has been a "wow"
I'm more than satisfied.
It's had its ups and downs I know
And it's highs and lows.

It's been rather like a fairground ride
With roundabouts and swings.
A Ferris wheel, a water slide
And perhaps the dodgems.

Music too has played its part
Swing. Jazz. The Proms and country style
All of these have touched my heart
At one time or another.

The future has a will of its own
Not for us to question
But from dawn to dusk
I give my thanks
For yet another day.
Whatever awaits
I'll do my best
And I'll do it my way.

Uncertainty

I am who I am
But who am I?

Think positive –
How can I think positive
When I don't know
What positive is anymore

Each time I turn around,
There's something in the way
Tearing at my heart,
It never goes away.

I feel like flotsam and jetsam
Swept along with the tide.
The tide of life –
My life – my tide

Whoever I am – whatever I am
I have a life to live.
If only I could find an answer
I would know for certain
Who I am – Without my man.

Goodbye

Oh, how sad we were today
When we said goodbye to Thornton House.
It has been a home from home
In every way
To our little band of O.A.P's

Senior Citizens we may be
But we call ourselves a family.
With years of wisdom
And a host of memories
Between us.

We have joined in our laughter
Shared in our tears
Lived again our golden years
But no more –
Under the roof of Thornton House.

Now we have a new home
Awaiting us
For how long we just don't know
But we will settle without a fuss
As one.

This new abode has been lent to us
By folks with Hearts Of Gold.
We know we're not young
But not too old
To enjoy life as it comes.

We thank our friends for this new beginning
May the Lord and his companions
Help us through these difficult times
With hope, we may, one day
Be happy under another Thornton House roof.

Cloud Watching

We all like to look up at the sky
And see the clouds as they float by
Fluffy on a bright sunny day
Gloomy and dull when rain is on its way

But these days there's more to see – Aeroplanes!
Now the world has expanded its horizons-
Thanks to the wealth of knowledge, far thinking
Of its aerodynamic "Boffins"

Every minute of every day there's
An aeroplane racing up there in the blue,
Criss crossing the clouds-
Leaving their flight path for all to see

I watch and I wonder at the pilot's skill
Maneuvering their craft, at will,
With dexterity and knowhow-
And me, left on mother earth, down below,
Quite spellbound!

Who are the passengers?
Are they outward bound?
Or on their way home from
A holiday or a business trip?
I will never know

I like my feet firmly on the ground
But it makes me wonder
How these magnificent flying machines
Stay up there, in the deep blue yonder!

A Sad Tale – (inspired by a piece of music)

Open the window –
It's another day –
It only makes me cry –
Why, Why, Why?
Poor old soul

Where will it all end?
Is there any end
To how I feel

I'm like a mole
Living in a hole
And it's dark, dark, dark.
Poor old soul

My hopes are useless
My wishes never come true
I just don't know any more –
Poor old soul

My body needs renewing
And my brain rewiring.
I'm just a mess, mess, mess.
Poor old soul

Recall

Remember all those happy days
When all we seemed to do was play?
Where did they all go, those happy times?
Of fairy tales and nursery rhymes?

We all have our dreams of days long gone
Of friends we knew, of Jane and John,
Where are they now, we often say
Are they remembering yesterday?

Forever fresh they come to mind
The present and the past entwined
In each of us there is a key –
It simply called us a memory.

Wild Flowers

On a very pleasant walk
Along the canal side, yesterday
I noticed the beauty of –
What we call weeds.
Not weeds, they are wild flowers!
Beauty abounding, beauty all their own.

Masses and masses. All varieties,
Scattered -, higgledy piggledy, -
Some entwined with others
Swaying in the breeze
Almost dancing.

The colours, -superb, a rainbow
Red, yellow, blue, pink, white.
Thistles too. Bearing their fluffy seeds
Almost ready to set them free.

Memories, memories, evoked
Memories of the blitz
Yes, there they were –
The 'Bomb Site Flowers"
A sad sight then
But no more.

Now, merrily adding to the vibrant picture
Of wild nature.
Alongside the Audlem Canal.

The Audlem Poetry Slam

A Poetry Slam – never heard of such a thing!
I said this to myself a few years ago
But now I know!

It is when poets have a great get together
Talk and read out loud, their own poetry –
To a very encouraging audience

They come, these poets,
From far and near.
They come, with great anticipation
Folders full of their creations.

Old and new, big or small
It really doesn't matter
As long as we all get along –
And we do – we all have a ball!

There are judges who know a thing or two
They know what they're about, -
Fair and square
The audience helps, with loud applause
Stamping their feet for extra praise.

I have even entered my meager endeavors
Which I've written with great thought
Not to win necessarily –
But to join in and enjoy
An evening "A little bit special"

Raindrops

From my kitchen window
I watched the raindrops
Gathering on my clothes line, outside.

It had been raining heavily –
For some hours.
Then the sun began to shine through
And brightened up my view.

The clothesline was laden with raindrops,
So I watched a while –
Kitchen chores forgotten!

One by one the raindrops raced –
Descending, with speed.
To the lowest point of the line.
Then, each time there was a collision,
One trembled, and fell to the ground.

Rather like "10 green bottles"
Not green bottles this time
But quivering, glittering little raindrops,
Glowing in the sun's early light.

In an instant – gone
And then there were none.

I try to see what I look at.

Despair

I'm out of work
Can't find a job
What will I do?
I'm not a yob
I have a mind

I do my best
I don't mind hard graft
I'm young and able
I'd learn a craft
Anything to put food on the table

I have a family
Young mouths to feed
They mean the world to me

They have a dad
What use is he?
Without a job
It's so sad –
I feel like a failure –

And it hurts.

Thought Provoking

Is there no end to the unrest in this world of ours?
No way out – no thought of peace
Peace among men, nation with nation
Suffering, heartache, hopelessness, despair
Always there

Life is so precious to us all, whoever we are
Young, old, colour, class or creed
And wherever we belong
So why oh why is there unrest
The need to kill and to destroy

There must be an answer, an understanding
But where do we begin?
For without a beginning, there will never be an end

To succeed, we must try, and try again
Reaching a final chapter – Peace
A peaceful world for our future generations

But without intelligent foresight
Peace cannot and will not be found
Then this world will cease to exist, end of life as we know it
For all

ABOUT THE AUTHOR

I was born in Bishop Auckland, County Durham in 1934 and spent the first 3 years of my life in Warminster, Wiltshire with my parents and older brother Keith before we all moved to Wembley in North London due to my Dad's work with the Post Office.

The war came along soon after, I can vividly remember watching the blitz from our front door and seeing the red sky as London suffered the bombing night after night. I can still picture the orange and red glow of the flames as they ate their way through everything in their path. The sights and smells along with the sound of the crackling of destruction are memories not easily forgotten.

After that I was one of the many children evacuated, however, I was fortunate to be sent to live with my Grandparents in Bishop Auckland for many many months.

I was pleased to go back to Wembley but then in 1944 a doodlebug fell on my School (Wembley Hill) which was at the end of road where we lived. Our house along with many in the neighbourhood lost its windows. Fortunately there were no casualties as the bomb landed during the early hours of a weekend.

Again I had to leave my loved ones and it was back to Bishop Auckland, this time to live with my Auntie Lillie. Being a little older, those months seemed to last forever and I missed my family very much. When I did rejoin them, of course there was no school to go to! I then spent a good deal of time attending other schools and even had some lessons in 'The Fifth Feathers Club' in Wembley along with all the other 'nomads'

A little after this, my brother joined the Royal Navy and left us, thankfully to return home safely a few years later. I did miss him during that time.

I met and married my first husband and moved house many times due to his employment as a civil and structural engineer. We had a lovely family and I made many friends each time we moved, eventually settling in Macclesfield, Cheshire.

Much later, I met and married my second husband settling back in the North East at Piercebridge, a village not very far from my birthplace and wartime evacuation location of Bishop Auckland. The house itself held many of its own secrets with not only the remains of a medieval monk being found in the garden but after an official excavation, the remnants and foundations of a Roman Bath House and a complete medieval church arch were discovered.

After my husband passed away, I came to live nearer some of my Children and Grandchildren in the beautiful village of Audlem on the Cheshire and Shropshire border. This is where I was encouraged to share some of my poetry through a poetry slam at the annual festival. This helped me settle and make many new friends in what is 'a great place to be'.

I have, and have had, a good life
Long may it last-
'Keep on writing'!

Jessie
November 2017

16374520R00055

Printed in Great Britain
by Amazon